College of Hawaii Publications
BULLETIN No. 1.

NOTES UPON HAWAIIAN PLANTS WITH DESCRIPTIONS OF NEW SPECIES AND VARIETIES.

BY

JOSEPH F. ROCK

HONOLULU:
PUBLISHED BY THE COLLEGE
DECEMBER, 1911.

In the interest of creating a more extensive selection of rare historical book reprints, we have chosen to reproduce this title even though it may possibly have occasional imperfections such as missing and blurred pages, missing text, poor pictures, markings, dark backgrounds and other reproduction issues beyond our control. Because this work is culturally important, we have made it available as a part of our commitment to protecting, preserving and promoting the world's literature. Thank you for your understanding.

NOTES UPON HAWAIIAN PLANTS WITH DESCRIPTIONS OF NEW SPECIES AND VARIETIES.

By Joseph F. Rock,
Botanist.

(Consulting Botanist, Board of Agriculture and Forestry.)

The writer has had opportunity of visiting all the high mountains of this island group with the exception of Mauna Loa, the second highest one.

The summits of these mountains, possessing as they do a temperate climate, harbor many interesting plants. Waialeale on Kauai 5080 feet, Puu Kukui on West Maui 5788 and Kaala, the summit of Kohala 5505 feet, are big open swamps. These are wrapped in clouds nearly the whole year round, with the exception of the short periods during which the south wind prevails. These swamps support a stunted vegetation consisting mainly of genera adapted to a moist and temperate climate.

Geraniums are to be found on all the high mountains with the exception of the summit of Kohala. Puu Kukui on West Maui and Waialeale on Kauai possess only small species which are very closely related, both of them being creepers a few inches high. On Mauna Kea, 13,823 feet, Hualalai, 8,969 feet, and Haleakala, 10,030 feet, they are stunted, some, however, reaching a height of 10 to 15 feet with a trunk of sometimes 7 inches in diameter; they do not, however, grow at an elevation higher than 10,000 feet. At 11,000 feet native vegetation ceases entirely, the only plant observed higher than that is *Sonchus oleraceus L.* with a long thick root-stock and prostrate leaves and flowers.

Viola is found on all the larger islands; none, however, had been recorded from the Island of Hawaii. During the month of June, 1910, the writer was fortunate to ascend to the summit of Kohala, where, to his surprise, he found a form of *Viola Maviensis* in the open bog. The plants are much taller than those from West Maui reaching a height of several feet. On East Maui the writer discovered a form of *V. robusta* growing in the dry sections on Haleakala, and on the island of Lanai a Viola similar to the one described by Forbes and Lydgate as *"Viola Helena;"* their plant came from the island of Kauai, mountains of Wahiawa.

Hillebrand, in his Flora of the Hawaiian Islands, mentions under Viola robusta, a plant collected by Remy on Lanai, No.

532, which he thought to be a variety of *V. robusta,* and also a plant collected by W. Knudsen on Kauai. The writer compared his specimens with Mr. Forbes' type and found them to be almost identical with the exception of variations in the leaves, and also differing in its single flowered peduncle; as a whole the plant is much taller than Forbes' type. The plant is decidedly distinct from *Viola robusta* and deserves the rank of species.

In addition to the notes on the genera *Viola* and *Geranium* the writer describes two new species of *Tetraplasandra;* one coming from the summit of Waialeale, the other from the island of Lanai.

This is the second species of that genus recorded from Kauai. *T. Waimeae* inhabiting the dry districts back of Waimea at an elevation of 3600 feet associated with *Sideroxylon sandwicense, Pterotropia Kauaiensis, Bobea Mannii, Solanum Kauaiense, Cyanea leptostegia,* etc., while *T. Waialealae* inhabits the swamps of the high plateau of Waialeale, elevation 5000 feet, in company with species peculiar to that region, such as *Drosera, Viola, Sanicula, Acaena, Geranium,* etc.

One species of *Pittosporum* is described from the island of Molokai; it being the only litoral species recorded from this archipelago, and a species of *Pelea* a handsome large tree from the lava fields of Auahi, Mt. Haleakala, elevation 2600 feet; it is remarkable for its habit of growth as a whole and for its large inflorescence which bears from 10-60 flowers.

At last a new species of *Sideroxylon* from the same locality as *Pelea multiflora* and a description of the fruits of *Sideroxylon spathulatum* hitherto unknown.

VIOLACEAE.

Viola L. Spec. pl. ed. 1 (1753) 933.

V. Maviensis Mann Enum. Haw. Pl. (1866) n. 11, et Fl. Haw. Isl. (1866) 120;—Hillebrand Fl. Haw. Isl. (1888) 16.

Maui: Summit of West Maui. Puu Kukui, elevation 5,788 feet, in bogy ground common in company with *Acaena exigua* Gray, *Geranium humile* Hbd. etc. (Rock n. 8148, flowering August 21, 1910). Also observed lower down at an elevation of 4600 feet.

Molokai: Swamp of Kawela near Kamoku camp, elevation 4,000 feet. (Rock n. 6106, fruiting, March, 1910).

Note: Only two small plants were observed in the open bog on Molokai in company with *Astelia* sp., *Selaginella deflexa* Brack., etc.

Var. **kohalana** Rock v. n. suffruticosa, caudicibus 10-16 dm longis, stipulis ovato-lanceolatis, foliis rotundatis in petiolos 7 cm longos; scapis 3-4 dm longis bibracteatis, pedicellis 3-9 cm longis, floribus magnis coeruleis vel albis.

Caudex 10-16 dm long, woody, more or less prostrate, stipules ovate lanceolate reddish brown, leaves as before on petioles of 2-7 cm, peduncles blackish blue when with dark blue flowers, light yellow, when with white flowers, bearing umbels of blue or white flowers on bibracteolate pedicels of 3-9 cm length; capsules as before.

Hawaii: Mountains of Kohala in bogy ground, mainly in thick moss on trees as well as near the summit of Kohala in open swampy places in company with *Cyathodes imbricata* var. *struthioloides, Selaginella deflexa*. etc. (Rock n. 8385, flowering and fruiting June 21, 1910). The flowers are very fragrant and large, the dark blue-flowered specimens occur lower down to an elevation of 4600 feet, while the white ones are found only higher up, 5200 feet elevation.

Note: This variety differs from the species in its very long caudex, scapes, and petioles, as well as pedicels and in its large flowers which are also white. No violets had been recorded, previously from the island of Hawaii.

V. Kauaensis Gray Bot. U. S. E. Exp. (1854) 85;—H. Mann Enum. Haw. Pl. n. 10, et Fl. Haw. Isl. (1866) 120;—Hillebr. Fl. Haw. Isl. (1888) 15;—Heller Pl. Haw. Isl. (1897) 857.

Kauai: Bog of Lehua makanoe, central plateau back of Kaholuamano, elevation 4200 feet. (Rock n. 2130, flowering March 8, 1909; Rock. n. 5723, fruiting Sept. 16, 1909). Also observed at Kauluwehi swamp, elevation 4300 feet, in company with *Drosera longifolia, Schizaea robusta*, etc., on Waialeale, the summit of Kauai, elevation 5250 feet, observed in company with *Sanicula, Acaena exigua, Dubautia waialealae*, etc.

Note: The specimens from Lehua makanoe are larger than those from Waialeale or Kauluwehi swamp.

Native names "Pohehiwa" and "Kalili."

V. robusta Hillebr. Fl. Haw. Isl. (1888) 16.

Molokai: Back of Kamoku camp on the banks of a stream, elevation 4000 feet, or less (Rock n. 6114, flowering and fruiting March, 1910; Rock n. 6196, on moss-covered tree trunks back of Kawela swamp, on the ridge leading to Pelekunu, flowering and fruiting March, 1910; Rock n. 7019 on tree trunks, heights above Kamalo ridge leading to Pelekunu, flowering and fruiting, April, 1910).

Note: Plants from above Kamalo are much smaller than those from Kamoku. The leaves of this plant are used medicinally by the natives, the same are boiled and the liquid drunk as tea.

Var. mauiensis Rock v. n. suffruticosus erectus, foliis oblongo-ovatis acuminatis subcordatis vel truncatis, serrulatis dentibus callosis, in petiolos hirsutos 1.5-2.5 cm longos, stipulis triangulatis acuminatis ciliatis; pedunculis hirsutis ex axillis foliorum. Capsula 1.5 cm longa; semina nigra ovoidea.

Habit as before, leaves with hirsute midribs, oblong ovate subcordate or truncate on hirsute petioles of 1.5-2.5 cm, stipules triangular from a broad base, accuminate, ciliate at the margins, the hirsute bibracteate peduncles 2-4 cm long one-flowered (never two) in the axils of every leaf, calyx hirsute linear lanceolate acuminate, flower buds only observed (petals pinkish); capsule 1.5 cm long, seeds ovoid blackish.

Maui: Gulches above Makawao slopes of Haleakala, elevation 3500 feet. (Rock n. 8563, fruiting October, 1910); southern slopes of Haleakala in a gulch near Kaupo Gap, elevation 5000 feet. (Rock n. 8686, fruiting November, 1910).

Note: Native name "Pamakani" on Maui; is used medicinally by the natives.

Var. **Wailenalenae** Rock v. n. Stem 1-2 m high, the branches as well as the stems hollow; stipules light brown, broadly lanceolate, acuminate about 3 cm long denticulate or serrate almost to the base; leaves thick, fleshy light green underneath darker above 9-10 cm x 3-4 cm ovate acuminate at both ends midrib as well as the 4 cm long petioles dark purple, serrulate with the base entire; flowers in the axils of the upper leaves single or two on a short bibracteate peduncle, pedicels 4-5 cm long bibracteolate above the middle; flowers nodding, sepals gibbous at the base 1 cm long, petals white not fragrant twice as long as the sepals, the lower one saccate, anthers appiculate, all winged, style curved thickening towards the stigma; capsule hirsute when young.

Kauai: High plateau of Waialeale along Wailenalena stream in shady places, elev. 4500 ft., not observed outside the banks of the stream. (Rock n. 8852, flowering and fruiting Oct. 21, 1911).

V. Helena Forbes var. **lanaiensis** Rock v. n. caule sufruticoso erecto, foliis oblongo-lanceolatis serratis breviter petiolatis, acuminatis, stipulis lanceolatis caudatis, fimbriatis, pedunculis ex axillis foliorum bi-bracteatis unifloriferis, petalis puniceis vel albis, sepala lanceolata, inferiore insaccato; capsula lanceolata, 12 mm longa, semina ovoidea, nigra.

Caudex erect 3 dm-13 dm long, woody, hollow, foliose at the apex, leaves oblong lanceolate, about 1 dm x 12-18 mm, acuminate at both ends, on somewhat margined petioles of 5 mm serrate with callous teeth, bluish purple when young, light green with pellucid oil dots when old, stipules lanceolate 1 cm long, caudate fimbriate, blackish, with a prominent median nerve; peduncles, bi-bracteate 1.5 cm with a bi-bracteolate pedicel of 4.5 cm long, bearing a single small, pinkish-white flower, sepals lanceolate not saccate. Capsule lanceolate 12 mm long, seeds ovoid blackish.

Lanai: Main ridge of Lanai. Lanai Hale and Haalelepakai, in bogy ground, elevation 3200 feet, terrestrial, (Rock n. 8046, flower buds and fruiting, July 25, 1910), also above Mauna Lei gorge on slopes above waterfall, elevation 2200 feet.

V. oahuensis Forbes Ocas. pap. B. P. Bishop Mus. IV. n. 3 (1909), p. 40.

Oahu: Dense forest on the windward side, Punaluu, back of Kaliuwaa, elevation 1800-2000 ft. (Rock n. 10 flowering July, 1908). (Rock and Forbes n. 359, flowering Nov. 14-21, 1908). (Rock n. 371, December 3-14, 1908, flowering, ridge above Kahana valley).

Note: This plant was first collected by the writer in July, 1908, and again during November 14-21, when in company with Mr. Forbes.

The plant is little distinct from V. robusta the common form on Molokai, it differs mainly in the stipules, which are 2-2.5 cm. long in my specimens, the white petals and the much smaller capsules, otherwise as in *V. robusta*.

V. Chamissoniana Gingins in Linnaea I. (1826) 408;—Gray U. S. E. Exp. (1854) 86 t. 6;—Walp. Report I., 216;—Mann Enum. Haw. Pl. (1866) n. 12, et Fl. Haw. Isl. (1866) 121;— Hillebr. Fl. Haw. Isl. (1888) 17;—Heller. Pl. Haw. Isl. (1897) 857. Includes V. trachelifolia Ging. l. c. p. 409.

Molokai: Back of Kamoku camp near Kawela swamps on the bank of a stream, elevation 4000 feet. (Rock n. 6113, flowering March, 1910), only one plant observed.

Note: The flowers are large and pink rather than pale purplish. The native name "Pamakani" applies to this species as well as to *V. robusta*.

Var. β Hillebrand Fl. Haw. Isl. (1888) 17.

Kauai: Outskirts of the forest below Kaholuamano, elevation 3000 feet. (Rock n. 2126, flowering and fruiting, March 3-10, 1909; and Oct. 22, 1911, flowering and fruiting).

Note: Young leaves are covered underneath with a silvery gray tomentum, old leaves pubescent.

Native name of the variety "Olopu" on Kauai.

GERANIACEAE.

Geranium L., Spec. pl. ed. 1 (1753) 676.
Sect. *Neurophyllodes* Gray.

G. arboreum Gray Bot. U. S. E. Exp. (1854) 315, t. 31;—H. Mann Enum. Haw. Pl. (1866) n. 63, et Fl. Haw. Isl. (1866) p. 163;—Hillebr. Fl. Haw. Isl. (1888) 57.

Maui: On the slopes of Haleakala, East Maui, in gulches near Puuniniau crater, elevation 6000-7000 feet; (Rock n. 8522, flowering and fruiting Oct., 1910), the plant grows in company with *Argyroxyphium virescens, Raillardia platyphylla,* etc.

Note: The flowers of this species are dark purple, with the petals unequal; it is a shrub with long rambling branches which are hirsute.

G. cuneatum Hook Icon. plant. (1840) t. 198;—Gray U. S. E. Exp. (1854) 312, t. 29;—Mann Enum. Haw. Pl. (1866) n. 61, et Fl. Haw. Isl. (1866) 162;—Hillebr. Fl. Haw. Isl. (1888) 55.

Hawaii: Slopes of Hualalai at an elevation of 6000 feet on a-a lava and black cinder (Rock n. 3589 flowering June 9, 1909), in company with *Raillardia, Cyathodes, Coprosma ernodeoides,* etc.

Note: The plants from Hualalai, probably the type locality, are not bushy but slender, erect 3-6 dm high and not as profusely branching as the variety from Mauna Kea; the young branches are reddish.

Var. *a.* Menziesii Hook. l. c.; Gray l. c.;—H. Mann Enum. Haw. Pl. (1866) n. 61, et Fl. Haw. Isl. (1866) 162;—Hillebr. Fl. Haw. Isl. (1888) 55 as synonyms.

Hawaii: Slopes of Mauna Kea, elevation between 9000-10,000 feet, above Kemole (Rock n. 8329, flowering June, 1910).

Note: This variety of *G. cuneatum* I observed only above Kemole on the western slopes of Mauna Kea, where it grew in company with several species of *Raillardia, Coprosma,* etc. The plant is very bushy and much branching, flowers whitish, leaves green on both sides, young branches not reddish as in the species.

Var. γ pauciflorum Hillbd. Fl. Haw. Isl. (1888) 55. Var. *hypoleucum* Gray U. S. E. Exp. (1854) 312, t. 29, in part.

Hawaii: Slopes of Mauna Kea above Waikii, elevation 10,000 feet. (Rock n. 8345, only one flowering specimen observed, May, 1910), (Hosmer n. 6081, Nov., 1909). (Hosmer n. 8700, flowering August, 1910).

Note: The plant has the habit of variety *a Menziesii* but differs in the canescent leaves. The flowering period of this variety falls in the late summer while the former flowers in May and June.

Geranium tridens Hillebr. Fl. Haw. Isl. (1888) 55. *G. cuneatum* Hook. var. γ *hololeucum* Gray U. S. E. Exp. (1854) 312 t. 29 D.;—H. Mann Enum. Haw. Pl. (1866) n. 61, et Fl. Haw. Isl. (1866) 162.

Maui: Slopes of Haleakala along the trail leading to the summit, elevation 6500-9000 feet. A very common shrub in company with *Sophora crysophylla, Raillardia Menziesii, Santalum Haleakalae*, etc. (Rock n. 8520 anl 8562, flowering and fruiting September, 1910, and October, 1910). (R. S. Hosmer n. 2620 April 26, 1909, without flowers and fruits).

Note: Native name Hinahina.

Geranium humile Hillebr. Fl. Haw. Isl. (1888) 56. *G. cuneatum* Hook. var. *hypoleucum* Gray U. S. E. Exp. (1854) 312 in part;—H. Mann Enum. Haw. Pl. (1866) n. 61, et Fl. Haw. Isl. (1866) 162.

Maui: Puu Kukui summit of West Maui, elevation 5788 feet. (Rock & Hammond n. 8147, flowering and fruiting August 21, 1910). Puu Kukui is an open flat swamp whose vegetation is mainly composed of the following species: *Acaena exigua, Lobelia Gaudichaudii, Viola mauiensis, Wilkesia Grayana, Cyathodes imbricata* var. *struthioloides, Lagenophora mauiensis*, besides a number of grasses and Cyperaceae.

Note: The large flowers of this species are not pure white as described by Hillebr., but have a pink center and purplish veins; usually three on a peduncle.

Var. **kauaiense** Rock var. nov. *G. cuneatum* var. Mrs. Sinclair's Indig. Fl. Haw. Isl. (1885) t. 35; planta 12 cm alta, foliis ovato-cuneatis, subtus argenteo-incanis, super viridibus glabris, apice 3-4 dentatis, dentibus callosis rubris, sepalis incanis.

Whole plant more slender than the species about 12 cm high; leaves smaller, ovate-cuneate, silky, canescent underneath, glabrous green above, the silkiness on the nerves is entirely wanting in the variety, dentate at the apex, with red callous teeth; usually 5-nerved; flowers smaller, pinkish white, mostly single or two on a peduncle, sepals silvery with a reddish border on the inner side, styles silvery tomentose up to the bright red stigmatic branches.

Kauai: Summit of Waialeale, elevation 5000 feet, on moss-covered rocks (Rock n. 4931, flowering Sept. 24, 1909, Oct. 20, 1911). Grows in company with *Dubautia waialealae, Sanicula sandwicensis* var., *Lobelia kauaensis, Drosera longifolia*, etc.

Note: The plant differs from the species in its smaller leaves which are glabrous above, and have reddish teeth, as well as in its styles, the bright red stigmatic branches are thick and not filiform as in *G. humile*.

Native name "Nohuanu."

ARALIACEAE.

Tetraplasandra Waialealae Rock sp. nov.

Arbor 6-8 m alta, ramis fatulis; foliis 30-45 cm longis, foliolis 5-9 oblongis acuminatis vel obtusis coriaceis, glabris, basi inequilateralibus, 9-14 cm x 4-5 cm, petiolulis 1-3 cm longis; inflorescentia umbellata composita terminalis; calyce 1.5 cm x 1 cm margine undulato, petalis 5-7; stamina numero petalorum quadrupla, 2-seriatis; ovarium 6-loculare; stigmata in stylopodia conica 5 mm alta.

A tree 6-8 m high with rather spreading branches, leaves 30-45 cm long; leaflets oblong acuminate, thick coriaceous unevensided at the base otherwise rounded; inflorescence a terminal compound umbel of usually 4 peduncles each about from 7-10 cm long, bearing 6 rays ca. 6 cm long, each bearing an umbellet of 2-5 pedicels ca. 2 cm long; calyx tubular purplish black with an undulate border; petals 5-7 triangular thick with a prominent median nerve, glabrous; stamens in two circles four times as many as petals, ovary 6-celled; stigmas on a conical stylopode of 5 mm.

Kauai: Summit of Waialeale, elevation 5000 feet, bordering the extensive bog, in company with *Dubautia, Pelea Waialealae, Suttonia lanceolata, Lobelia kauaensis, Labordea Waialealea*, etc. It grows at the edge of a cliff overlooking the windward side of Kauai, as well as along the banks of Kaluiti stream, and at the summit proper. (J. F. Rock n. 4902 (young fruits), Sept. 22, 1909, and n. 8870 flowering Oct. 20, 1911; type in Herbarium College of Hawaii).

PLATE I.

Tetraplasandra Waialealae. Rock.
About one half natural size; showing flower buds and open flowers.

Tetraplasandra Lanaiensis Rock sp. nov.

Arbor 5 m alta, prorsus glabra; foliis 30-38 cm longis, foliolis 5-7, oblongis, obtusis vel breviter acuminatis, basi inequilateralibus, in petiolulos 1 cm-1.5 cm longos, petiolulo foliolii terminalis multo longiore, articulato; inflorescentia ter umbellata in rachem communem 2.5 cm longam; calyce ca. 6 mm, margine denticulato, petalis 5-6 lanceolatis viridi-flavidis, 7 mm longis, stamina numero petalorum dupla, ovarium 3-loculare, stigmata sessilis.

A small tree about 5 m high, branching freely, bark smooth writish, glabrous throughout; leaves 30-38 cm long, leaflets 5-7 oblong, obtuse or bluntly acuminate, unevensided at the base, midrib prominent, 8-10 cm x 4-5 cm, dark green above light underneath, the terminal leaflet on a petiolule of 4 cm which is articulate near the blade, the lateral ones on petiolules of 1-1.5 cm, subcoriaceous; inflorescence thrice umbellate not erect but drooping, the 3-5 peduncles on a common rhachis of about 2.5 cm, about 20 cm long, bearing umbels of 17-21 slender drooping rays of 8-10 cm, these again umbellate with 7-13 pedicels; calyx tubular ca. 6 mm with a denticulate border, petals 5-6 lanceolate greenish-yellow, 7 mm long, stamens twice as many as petals, ovary 3-celled, stigmas sessil.

Lanai: Dry forehills in Mahana valley, not common, only two trees observed, associated with *Osmanthus sandwicensis, Suttonia Lanaiensis, Sideroxylon spathulatum, Maba sandwicensis*, etc. (Rock n. 8088 flowering August 2, 1910); type in Herbarium College of Hawaii.

PLATE II.

Tetraplasandra Lanaiensis Rock.
Less than half natural size.

RUTACEAE.

Pelea multiflora Rock sp. nov.

Arbor 10-15 m alta, ramis robustis; folia opposita, 10-20 cm x 5-9 cm, petiolata petiolis hirsutis 2-4 cm longis, oblonga, obtusa, basi subcordata, supra glabra, subtus tomento olivaceo praesertim in nervo mediano prominente induta; inflorescentia hirsuta cymoso-paniculata 10-12 cm longa, flores 10-60; calycis lobi ovati acuti petalis longiores, petala et ovaria glabra, capsula glabra quadriloba.

A tall tree 10-15 m high with very stout branches; leaves opposite oblong 10-20 cm x 5-9 cm, glabrous above, densely covered underneath with an olivaceous tomentum, especially along the prominent midrib and nerves; marginal nerve wanting; young leaves golden yellow densely hirsute; inflorescence cymosely paniculate 10-12 cm long, hirsute throughout, with 5-6 nodes, the common peduncle 2-3 cm with large lanceolate bracts of 1.5 cm under the lower cymose branches of usually 6 cm in length with three or four nodes, ultimate pedicels 5 mm long, bearing from 10-60 flowers, floral bracts subulate enclosing the persistent calyx which in turn encloses the 4-valvate petals of 5 mm in the fertile flowers; sepals ovate acute hirsute, petals and ovary glabrous; capsule glabrous 3 cm each way, carpels parted their entire length.

Maui: Haleakala, lavafields of Auahi, district of Kahikinui, in company with *Alectryon macrococcus, Pterotropia dipyrena, Bobea sandwicensis, Alphitonia excelsa, Antidesma pulvinatum,* etc. (Rock n. 8646 flowering and fruiting Nov., 1910).

PLATE III.

Pelea multiflora Rock.

PITTOSPORACEAE.

Pittosporum halophylum Rock sp. nov.

Frutex erectus ca 1 m altus, rami robusti; folia coriacea, ovata vel obovata 4-6.5 cm x 2-3 cm, breviter petiolata petiolo 1 cm longo, obtusa vel emarginata, basi breviter acuminata, supra glabra, pallide viridia, subtus flavido-fusco-tomentosa; inflorescentia caulina, sepala oblonga, acuminata, tomento sericeo flavido induta; corollae cremeae tubus 1 cm laciniis 3-polo longior; ovarium hirsutum; capsula (ignota).

A small shrub ca 1 m high, with stout branches; leaves ovate to obovate, 4 cm-6.5 cm x 2 cm-3.3 cm, obtuse or rounded or emarginate at the apex suddenly tapering into a short petiole of 1 cm, pale green above wrinkled with a close areolar network, glabrous, covered with a yellowish brown wool underneath, young leaves pubescent on both sides; inflorescence cauline immediately under the leaves, on a short peduncle of 5 mm; flowers on pedicels of 5 mm, covered with a fawn colored tomentum, corolla cream colored fragrant, tube 1 cm, petals one third as long; stamens two-thirds the length of the tube, anthers oblong; ovary hirsute, style as long as the tube; capsule unknown.

Molokai: Along the beach on the windward side of the island within the spray of the sea, between Kalawao and Waikolu, (Rock & Nevin n. 6183 flowering March 26, 1910; Nevin flowering Aug. 14, 1911). This species is exceedingly interesting as it represents the only litoral species from the islands; the name P. litorale was used at first in the manuscript, but having been anticipated for a Philippine species by Merrill, the Greek name is here substituted for it.

PLATE IV.

Pittosporum halophylum Rock.
About one half the natural size.

SAPOTACEAE.

Sideroxylon auahiense Rock sp. nov.

Arbor 8-10 m alta, folia coriacea glabra, folia novella tomentosa, elliptico-oblonga 8-12 cm longa, 4-6 cm lata petiolis 3-4 cm longis; flores solitarii vel 2 ex axillis foliorum; ovarium villosum 5-loculare, bacca globosa, citrea, apice acuminata, sessilis vel subsessilis 3.5cm-4.5 cm diam.

A tree 8-10 m high, with a broad round crown, branches pale glaucous, terete ,glabrous; leaves coriaceous pale green glabrous on both sides when old, shining above, covered with a gray silvery tomentum when young, elliptical oblong, bluntly acuminate or rounded, 8-12 cm x 4-6 cm on petioles of 3-4 cm, veins parallel leaving midrib at wide angles of about 80°; flowers single, rarely two in the axilis of the alternate leaves, calyx hirsute 5 parted to near the base, the lobes rounded, corolla (?); ovary hirsute five celled, style short, berry drupaceous sessil or subsessil bright citron yellow smooth globose pointed at the apex, five seeded 3.5 cm-4-5 cm in diameter, bright yellow inside, fleshy; seeds 20 mm long by 10 mm wide, enclosed in a thin papery pyrena, elongate not flat as in *S. rhynchospermum*, the thick crustaceous testa yellowish with reddish spots, shining; the scar of the raphe shorter than the ventral angle; cotyledons as broad and long as the albumen the minute radical inferior.

The tree differs from *S. sandwicense* mainly in its large bright yellow sessil fruits which have the shape of the fruits of the African Mangosteen, in its single flowers, and very pale glabrous foliage.

Maui: Southern slopes of Haleakala lava fields at Auahi, district of Kahikinui, elevation 3000 feet, in company with *Alectryon macrococcus, Pelea multiflora, Pterotropia dypirena*, etc. *Sideroxylon sandwicense* var? is found also at the same place, having fruits exactly like *S. rhynchospernum*, but seeds as in *S. sandwicense*. *Sideroxylon spathulatum* only recorded from Lanai grows also at Auahi, Maui, but 1000 feet or so lower than *S. auahiense*, in company with *Chrysophyllum polynesicum*. (Rock no. 8668 fruiting Nov., 1910). Type Herb. College of Hawaii.

The specific name refers to the locality on Haleakala to which the tree is peculiar.

PLATE V.

Sideroxylon auahiense Rock.
Less than half natural size.

Sideroxylon spathulatum Hbd.

Flora Haw. Isl. (1888) 277;—Drake Del Castillo, Illust. Fl. Insul. Maris Pacifici (1892) 228.

The fruits of this species, which were unknown, were collected by the writer in company with Mr. J. G. Hammond on the island of Lanai where the tree is quite common. Following is a description of the fruits of the above species:

Fruit a drupaceous berry dark orange colored and glabrous when mature, covered with a rufous tomentum when young, 3.5 cm long, by little over 2 cm wide, conical, acuminate at the apex; 5-seeded, each seed enclosed in a membraneous yellow pyrena, 20 mm long, 7 mm wide, rounded at both ends, grayish brown, rather dull, linear elongate, the raphe occupying almost the whole ventral angle. Cotyledons nearly as long and broad as the albumen, radical about 3 mm long and superior, fruit flesh light yellow.

Lanai: Common in Mahana and Kaiholena Valley as well as on the windward slopes of Lanai in company with *Chrysophyllum polynesicum, Bobea sandwicensis, Osmanthus,* etc. (Rock n. 8039 flowering and fruiting July 26, 1910).

Maui: Southern slopes of Haleakala lava fields of Auahi, Kahikinui, elevation 2000 feet. (Rock no. 8684 fruiting November, 1910). In company with *Reynoldsia sandwicensis, Antidesma pulvinatum,* etc.

Printed by Libri Plureos GmbH in Hamburg, Germany